DNA Analysis: Forensic Fluids & Follicles

by Sue Hamilton

VISIT US AT
WWW.ABDOPUBLISHING.COM

Published by ABDO Publishing Company, 8000 West 78th Street, Suite 310, Edina, Minnesota 55439.
Copyright ©2008 by Abdo Consulting Group, Inc. International copyrights reserved in all countries.
No part of this book may be reproduced in any form without written permission from the publisher.
ABDO & Daughters™ is a trademark and logo of ABDO Publishing Company.

Printed in the United States.

Editor: John Hamilton
Series Consultant: Scott Harr, J.D. Criminal Justice Dept Chair, Concordia University St. Paul
Graphic Design: Sue Hamilton
Cover Design: Neil Klinepier
Cover Illustration: iStockphoto
Interior Photos and Illustrations: p 1 Scientist, Comstock; p 3 DNA strand, iStockphoto; p 4 DNA strand, Getty; p 5 Forensic scientist, AP; p 6 Vials with red liquid, Comstock; Fingerprint & DNA strand, Comstock; p 7 Dr. Jeffreys, AP; p 8 DNA printout, Getty; p 9 Using a swab to collect DNA, Getty; p 10 DNA chart from 1989, Getty; p 11 Examining a DNA profile, AP; p 12 Blood test for DNA, AP; p 13 DNA testing results, Corbis; p 14 Microscope with DNA background, Comstock; p 15 Gloved hand & vials of blood, iStockphoto; DNA profile, ©2002 Regents of the University of Michigan; pp 16-17 FBI's CODIS announcement, AP; p 18 DNA swab, iStockphoto; Technician opens evidence bag, AP; p 19 Hair follicle in tweezers, AP; Tooth held by technician, Getty; p 20 Gloved hand with vial, iStockphoto; Photos of Nicole Brown Simpson, Ronald Goldman, & O.J. Simpson, AP; p 21 Police at the Simpson/Goldman crime scene, AP; p 22 Glove found at O.J. Simpson's estate, AP; O.J. Simpson, AP; p 23 O.J. Simpson's home, AP; p 24 Bloody glove, AP; p 25 Judge Ito examines DNA printout, AP; p 26 Hand holding test tube of fluid, iStockphoto; p 27 O.J. Simpson found not guilty, AP; p 28 A forensic scientist processes DNA, AP; p 29 James Tillman and Karen Goodrow, AP; p 31 Swabbing for DNA, iStockphoto.

Library of Congress Cataloging-in-Publication Data

Hamilton, Sue L., 1959-
   DNA analysis : forensic fluids & follicles / Sue Hamilton.
      p. cm. -- (Crime scene investigation)
   Includes index.
   ISBN-13: 978-1-59928-987-8
   1. Forensic genetics--Juvenile literature. 2. DNA--Analysis--Juvenile literature. 3. DNA fingerprinting--Juvenile literature. I. Title.
   RA1057.5.H36 2008
   572.8'6--dc22
                              2007035157

CONTENTS

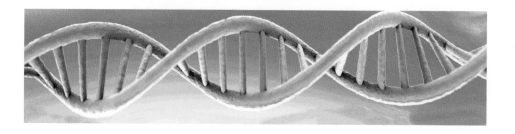

Forensic Fluids & Follicles

Did you use your toothbrush today? Did you brush or comb your hair? Is there a bandage in the trash with some of your blood on it? If so, your Deoxyribonucleic Acid (DNA) is on every one of those items and dozens of others in your home and at your school. DNA is found in saliva, hair root follicles, and blood, as well as in sweat, urine, semen, skin, fingernails—nearly every part of a person.

Below: A strand of DNA, which contains the genetic instructions for the development and function of living organisms.

First discovered in 1868 by Swiss physician Friedrich Miescher, DNA is known as the blueprint of life. In living things, DNA is the material inside the center of every cell that forms genes. This material is inherited from an individual's parents. Except for identical twins, whose DNA is identical, every person's DNA is different.

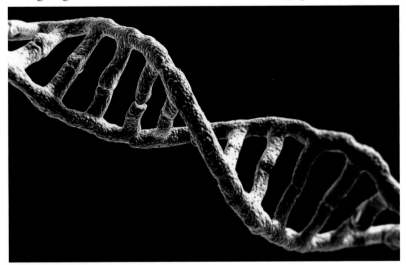

For forensic scientists, DNA is a miracle tool. The word "forensic" is defined as using science and technology to investigate a crime and provide facts in a court of law.

Today, DNA analysis helps law enforcement agencies identify people involved at crime scenes. From a tiny drop of blood on a car door to skin cells collected from under a murder victim's fingernails, this technology is often used to help prove a suspect's guilt or innocence.

Above: A crime lab forensic scientist uses a swab to collect DNA from a shirt.

DNA Fingerprinting Discovered

Studies in the 1950s found that a large part of the DNA pattern holds species-specific traits—the same information from human-to-human or animal-to-animal or plant-to-plant. It is why humans have feet instead of hooves or roots. Scientists knew that a large portion of one person's DNA was the same as every other human's DNA. However, in September 1984, a brilliant discovery showed differences in DNA patterns.

British geneticist Dr. Alec Jeffreys and his associates at the University of Leicester in Leicester, England, found that fragments of each person's DNA are unique to that person. Jeffreys said, "It was a 'eureka!' moment." A few months later, in 1985, the scientist announced what he called "DNA fingerprinting" to the world. Scientists could identify someone from a small sample of that person's tissues or fluids.

Almost immediately, DNA's use in forensic investigations was clear. Since nearly all of the estimated 10 trillion cells in a human body contain the same genetic information, a sample from nearly any part of a person can identify that person. A cell from a person's skin or hair roots will have the same genetic information as a cell from that person's sweat, saliva, urine, and blood.

Below: "DNA fingerprinting" was discovered in 1984.

Evidence from a crime scene could be collected and then analyzed to identify a thief or a killer. It wouldn't be long before Jeffreys had his first opportunity to use DNA fingerprinting.

Above: Alec Jeffreys holds a copy of the first DNA fingerprint profile.

First Use Of DNA Analysis

Dr. Alec Jeffreys' work was first tested in an immigration case. A family from London, England, had a son who traveled to Ghana, West Africa. The young man was on his way home to the United Kingdom when immigration officials stopped him. They thought his passport was a fake, and that he was an imposter.

Jeffreys said, "We took the case on—and it was a tricky case. The woman had sisters back in Ghana, so the boy could have been a nephew, and we didn't have the father for analysis. All we had were three fully accepted children—so we used these children to reconstruct the DNA fingerprint of the missing father."

Jeffreys compared the DNA of the boy with the other family members' DNA. When the scientist had completed the DNA fingerprinting, he found the boy was definitely the British family's son. The case was dropped and the boy was allowed to return home.

News of DNA's use in proving identity made headlines around the world. Suddenly, Professor Jeffreys and his associates were flooded with calls from thousands of families facing similar problems. DNA analysis was a success.

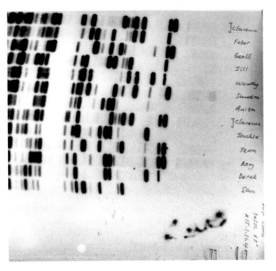

Below: A DNA fingerprinting chart for a family, including the mother, father and nine children.

Above: A swab is used to collect DNA from inside a person's mouth.

DNA Fingerprinting & Profiling

Below: An analyst examines DNA charts in 1989. Law enforcement officials use DNA evidence to identify people involved in crime scene investigations.

From the start, immigration and proving fatherhood were important issues that DNA analysis solved. Crime scene investigators found DNA's greatest use to be in identifying individuals involved in criminal cases. However, DNA fingerprinting was a complex process. Also, some professionals felt that the term "DNA fingerprinting" might make people think that DNA analysis was associated with fingerprint analysis. Both DNA and fingerprint analysis are unique to each individual, but the identification processes are quite different.

Professor Jeffreys felt that if DNA analysis was to be used as forensic proof, it would need to be simplified. The complicated patterns were difficult to explain in court. Jeffreys developed a slightly different approach: DNA profiling.

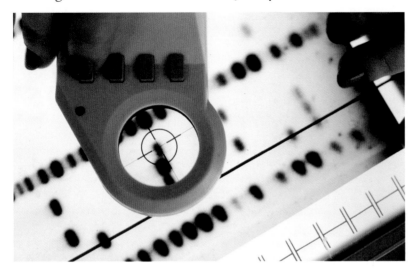

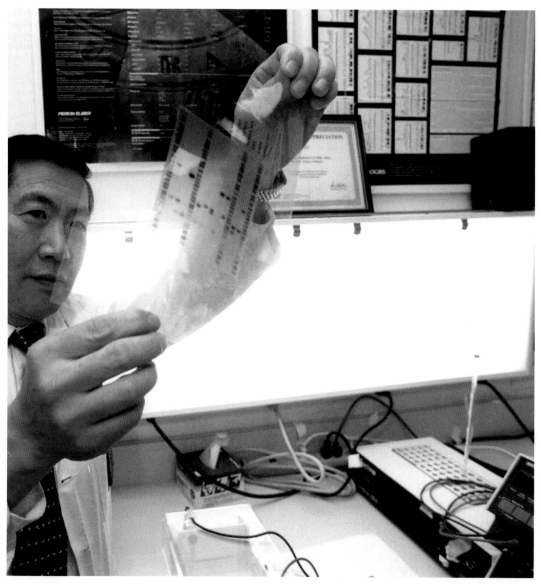

Minisatellites are sections of repeated DNA that are used as genetic markers to identify an individual. DNA profiling focused on minisatellites that were the most different. Jeffreys' use of DNA profiling, also called DNA typing, DNA analysis, or DNA matching, became a vital forensic science tool. It would not be long before the scientist would be asked to use his knowledge of DNA profiling to help find and convict a killer.

Above: The head of a forensics lab examines a DNA profile. Criminal profiles are kept and loaded into a computer database.

Clearing the Innocent

In 1986, only a year after announcing his findings to the world, Jeffreys was asked to help in a criminal investigation taking place only 12 miles (19 km) from his lab. Two 15-year-old girls had been raped and strangled in the town of Narborough, Leicestershire, England. The first girl, Lynda Mann, had died in 1983. Semen was collected from the girl's body. Analysis told police that the killer was blood type A. No other clues were found, and the case went unsolved.

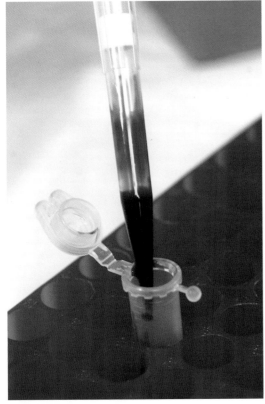

Below: Blood is placed in a tube for DNA testing.

Three years later, a second girl, Dawn Ashworth, met the same horrifying fate. Her killer was also blood type A. Police were sure that one person had committed both crimes. Officers arrested Richard Buckland, a local 17-year-old boy. The teen only confessed to the rape of the second girl. Although mildly mentally challenged, Buckland seemed to know enough about the second case to prove that he was responsible for the crime. Convinced that the young man had raped and killed both girls, the police asked Professor Jeffreys to conduct a DNA analysis between semen found in each of the victims and a sample of the suspect's blood.

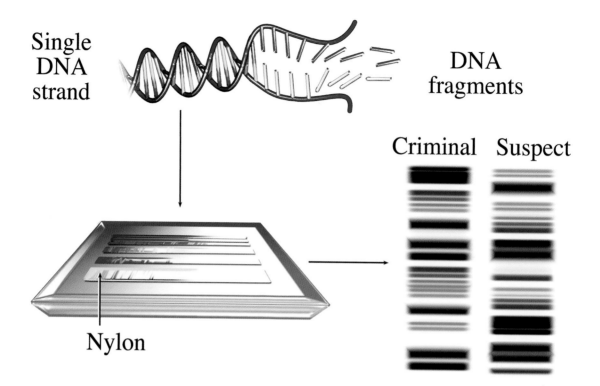

Single
DNA
strand

DNA
fragments

Criminal   Suspect

Nylon

Jeffreys went to work. He came back with an answer, but it was not the one police were expecting. Jeffreys said, "The police were right—both girls had been raped by the same man. But it wasn't the man who confessed."

To double-check the DNA results, Dr. Peter Gill and Dr. Dave Werrett of the Forensic Science Service (FSS) also conducted the tests. Gill and Werrett had worked with Jeffreys previously, publishing a paper on how DNA profiling could be used in forensic investigations. Gill said, "Since the technique had not been used in criminal casework before, the FSS were asked by the police to confirm Dr. Jeffreys' conclusions."

Gill and Werrett's tests confirmed that Buckland was innocent. Said Jeffreys, "He had given a false confession and was released—so the first time DNA profiling was used in criminology, it was to prove innocence."

Above: DNA testing results. The illustration shows how a single strand of DNA can be used as evidence in a criminal case. The criminal and the suspect's DNA do not match.

The First DNA-Based Manhunt

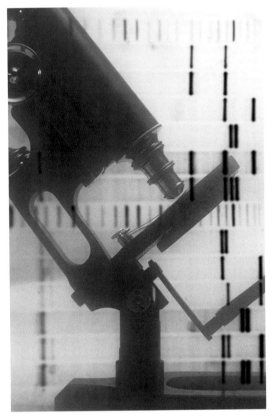

On November 21, 1986, DNA analysis proved that Richard Buckland wasn't the killer of two girls in the town of Narborough. Why had Buckland confessed? It may have been because he was confused or afraid. Buckland might have accidentally stumbled across Dawn Ashworth's body, which allowed him to know details no one else knew. However, Buckland's innocence and false confession meant that a killer was still on the loose in this small community.

Armed with the perpetrator's DNA profile, police began the world's first DNA-based manhunt in 1987. Blood samples were collected from 5,511 males between the ages of 13 and 34.

Left: Hundreds of hours were spent collecting and testing DNA samples in 1987 during the world's first DNA manhunt.

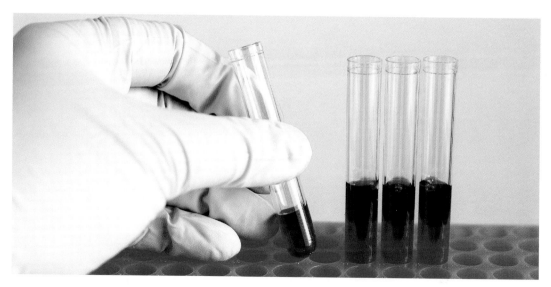

Testing showed that 10 percent of the men had blood type A—the same as the killer's. Now began the work of testing hundreds of DNA samples. Each test took days to complete. For months, DNA testing continued. No matches were found. Then the police got a break.

A woman in a bar overheard a local bakery worker, Ian Kelly, drunkenly say that he had provided his blood sample in place of his co-worker's, Colin Pitchfork. Kelly lived outside of the manhunt area, so he hadn't been asked to provide a blood sample. Pitchfork claimed that his previous run-ins with the law would cause him to be treated badly by the police. Pitchfork convinced Kelly to stand in for him.

Police immediately arrested Colin Pitchfork. His blood test revealed a complete DNA match with the samples taken from the murdered girls. Pitchfork was the killer. The first DNA-based manhunt resulted in the murderer receiving a life sentence.

DNA analysis saved an innocent man and identified the criminal. Jeffreys said, "This man would have killed again, no doubt about it. DNA testing helped save lives." Forensic science had a huge tool in its fight for truth.

Above: Vials of blood ready for testing.
Below: An autoradiograph showing DNA profiles. There is a match of the DNA profile of defendant 1 and the forensic sample.

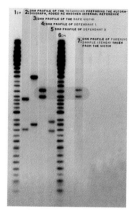

Collecting & Using DNA Evidence

Right: An FBI official announces the Combined DNA Index System (CODIS) in a 1998 news conference. More than 10 years later, nearly 5 million convicted offenders' DNA profiles are in the database. Law enforcement officers are able to compare genetic evidence taken from convicted felons and gathered in unsolved cases.

Since the late 1980s, DNA collection became a standard part of crime scene investigation. In 1990, the Federal Bureau of Investigation (FBI) began a project that allowed collected DNA analyses to be placed in a database. By 1994, the FBI's Combined DNA Index System (CODIS) was formally established. Four years later, the system was made available to law enforcement agencies across the country. CODIS allows searches of known criminals' DNA. It also holds DNA profiles of unknown suspects who may have committed crimes in different areas. Nearly five million convicted offenders' DNA profiles are in the database.

Collecting DNA evidence is an important part of a crime scene investigator's job. All types of fluids and follicles are carefully collected, packaged, preserved, and documented. Strict guidelines for collecting and transferring evidence are to be followed.

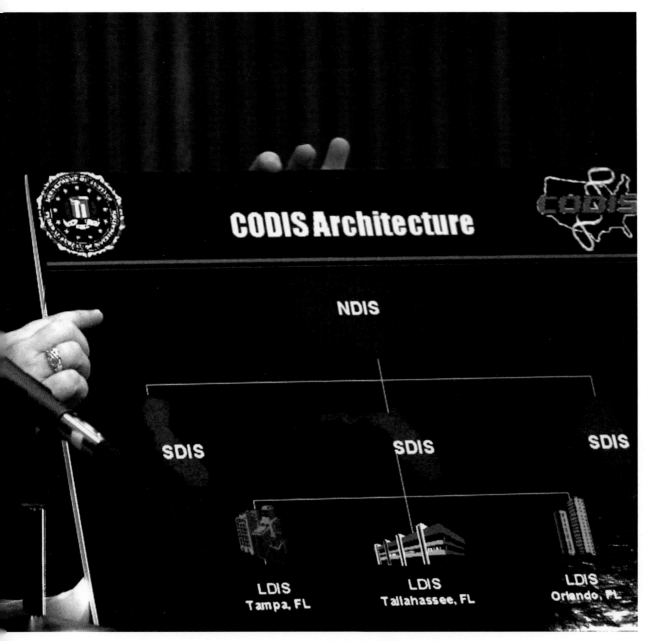

Every piece of evidence has a "chain of custody" form attached. Anyone who receives the evidence must sign the form and be able to prove that no one else had access to the evidence. Breaking any of the rules could result in the evidence being found unusable in court, which means a criminal might go free.

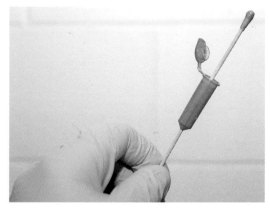

Above: A swab is used to collect DNA.

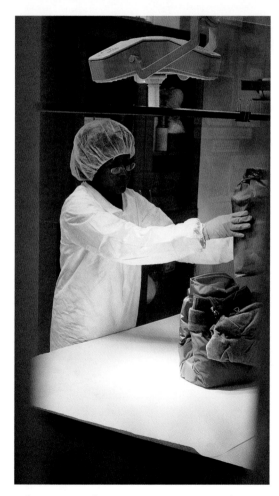

Above: A technician removes a jacket from a sealed evidence bag in a crime lab examination room.

Extreme care is taken with all DNA samples. A sneeze or cough from anyone who comes in contact with a sample can contaminate it with that person's DNA. Even touching a person's eyes, mouth, or nose, and then touching the area where the evidence will be placed, can add another DNA sample. Contaminated DNA samples do not hold up in court.

Fluids

Blood, saliva, sweat, urine, and semen may be found on a victim, on surrounding items (clothing, bedding, towels, etc.), or surfaces (floors, walls, counters, etc.). The fluid may be wet or it may have dried. If the fluid is wet, a clean cotton cloth or a swab (which looks like a common Q-tip) is used to collect a sample. This sample is then allowed to air-dry. Fluids collected from snow or pools of water are analyzed immediately. Too much water will dilute the fluid, and the DNA information will be lost. For dried evidence, the swab is moistened with distilled water and then wiped across the dried fluid. The collected swabs or items are allowed to air-dry, and then individually sealed in paper envelopes and transported to the crime lab. Paper envelopes or bags are nearly always used for transporting this type of evidence. Paper is a porous material that allows air exchange and helps keep the DNA undamaged.

Follicles

Hair follicles are carefully picked up with clean forceps or gloved fingers. Crime scene investigators must protect the hair's root tissue. This bulb-like part of the hair, which begins just

under the skin, holds the DNA information. Hair without the root tissue does not contain DNA. If the hair is mixed with body fluids, it is allowed to air-dry. Once collected, it is then packed and sealed in a clean paper envelope and submitted to the lab.

Above: A hair follicle is held with a tweezers at a crime lab.
Below: A lab technician holds a tooth that will be swabbed for DNA.

Tissues

Evidence such as skin, muscle, and organs are picked up with clean forceps or gloved fingers. These types of samples are sealed in clean, airtight plastic containers for prompt transfer to the lab.

Bones and Teeth

Bones and teeth are placed in clean paper envelopes or bags, and then sealed.

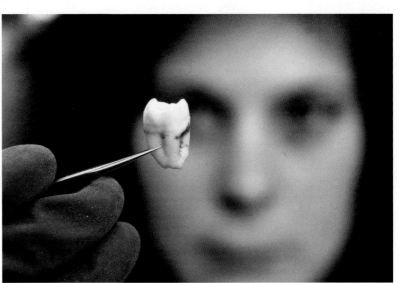

The Simpson/ Goldman Murders

Whenever possible, DNA is collected from victims, as well as anyone who may have been in close contact with the victims—family members, close friends, co-workers, boyfriends, girlfriends, etc. This process rules out some people, while helping investigators decide who to focus on more closely. One of the most famous DNA evidence cases of the 20th century involved a well-known ex-husband whose DNA turned him into a prime suspect.

On June 12, 1994, Nicole Brown Simpson and Ronald Goldman were brutally stabbed to death outside of Nicole's home in a wealthy area of Brentwood, California. Nicole was the ex-wife of O.J. Simpson, a former professional football player and actor. Ron Goldman was a waiter at a local restaurant. He had stopped to return a pair of glasses that had been left at the restaurant that night by Nicole's mother.

Above: Nicole Brown Simpson. Ron Goldman. O.J. Simpson.

Nicole's dog, barking and running free, led neighbors to make the grisly discovery around midnight that Sunday evening. The police were called, and within minutes the area was sealed off. Blood pools, spatters, and trails surrounded the two victims and the immediate area.

Above: Crime scene investigators collect evidence from Nicole Brown Simpson's Brentwood, California, home on June 13, 1994.

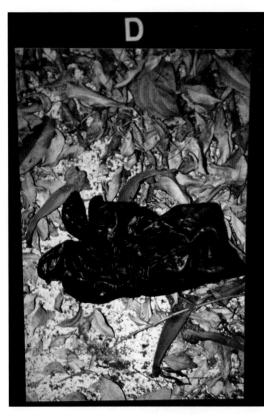

Above: An evidence photo of the right-hand glove found at O.J. Simpson's home.
Below: O.J. Simpson leaves the police station after being questioned on June 13, 1994.

Simpson's children, eight-year-old daughter Sydney and five-year-old son Justin, were asleep in their rooms in the townhouse. Whoever had attacked Nicole and Ron had not entered Nicole's home to steal and had not disturbed the sleeping children. A murderer was loose in the area.

O.J. Simpson's home was only a few miles away from Nicole's townhouse. Detectives arrived at the home, planning to notify O.J. of his ex-wife's murder. When no one answered either the door or the phone, officers became concerned. They noticed bloodstains on a Ford Bronco parked nearby. A quick check showed that the vehicle had been leased to Simpson.

Fearing that O.J. had also been attacked, police entered O.J.'s estate without a search warrant. They met Brian "Kato" Kaelin, a friend of Simpson's who was staying in O.J.'s guesthouse. He told the officers of hearing noises earlier that evening. Police searched the grounds and found a glove. It seemed to match another glove found at the Simpson/Goldman crime scene.

Above: O.J. Simpson's 1994 Brentwood, California home. On the night that Nicole Brown Simpson and Ronald Goldman were found dead, when no one answered the doorbell at the house, police entered the estate and found a glove that seemed to match a bloody glove at the Simpson/Goldman crime scene.

Police also met with O.J.'s 25-year-old daughter, Arnelle, who was living with her father. Arnelle informed officers that O.J. had flown to Chicago, Illinois, a few hours earlier to attend a celebrity golf tournament.

O.J. was finally contacted in Chicago at 5:00 AM that morning. He immediately flew back to California. However, it would be only a few days later that O.J. would go from shocked and grieving ex-husband to the main suspect in this double-murder case.

DNA Wars

On the morning of June 13, 1994, blood was collected from several sources at the Simpson/Goldman murder scene. This included blood from the bodies of Nicole and Ron, as well as a bloodstained leather glove left at the scene, and blood drops found several steps away from the bodies. Investigators believed the blood drops must have come from a cut on the killer's left hand.

Because a glove and bloodstains were seen by police at the O.J. Simpson estate, a search warrant was obtained for O.J.'s home. Police collected the right-hand glove, which seemed a match for the left-hand one found at the crime scene. O.J.'s Ford Bronco was taken into police custody. Blood samples were collected from outside and inside the vehicle. Samples were also collected of a blood trail leading up to O.J.'s front door and into the house. Dark socks were collected, but it wasn't until later that they were found to contain bloodstains.

Right: DNA testing was conducted on the bloodstained left-hand glove found at the murder scene of Nicole Brown Simpson and Ronald Goldman.

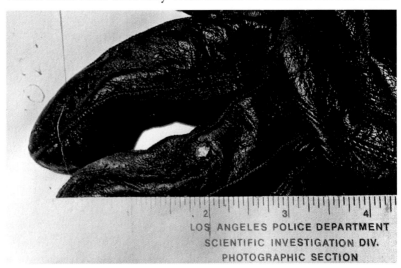

LOS ANGELES POLICE DEPARTMENT
SCIENTIFIC INVESTIGATION DIV.
PHOTOGRAPHIC SECTION

O.J. returned to his home just before noon on June 13. It was noted that Simpson had cuts and scratches on his left hand and a bandage on his middle finger. O.J. was asked to go to police headquarters to provide blood for DNA testing. He did so voluntarily. However, his blood sample was not delivered directly to the lab. Instead, Detective Philip Vannatter pocketed the vial of blood and carried it back to Simpson's home, delivering it to Dennis Fung, the head criminalist in charge of collecting evidence. Detective Vannatter would later be accused of planting drops of O.J.'s blood at the crime scene. Vannatter denied the charge. However, this was one of several glaring mistakes that occurred during the processing of the Simpson/Goldman crime scene.

Above: Judge Lance Ito, who presided over the 1995 Simpson murder trial, holds a sample of an autoradiology picture of DNA sequences, small bars that illustrate the genetic patterns of a person's blood.

On the day of the murder, Nicole's body was respectfully covered with a blanket taken from her home. Although meant to protect the family from the massive media coverage taking place all around the area, the result was contamination of the crime scene. Also, no blood was collected that day from stains on the fence's back gate, where the killer exited. A sample was collected several weeks later, but by then the crime scene was no longer secure. Another issue occurred when the technicians collecting the blood went from the crime scene to O.J. Simpson's home and back to the crime scene, keeping some of the collected samples stored in a hot lab truck for as long as seven hours. It was argued that the heat ruined the samples.

Above: When handling a blood sample, technicians must wear sterile latex gloves at all times to avoid contaminating the evidence. This was one of the errors that occurred during the processing of the Simpson/Goldman crime scene evidence.

Several other collection errors occurred, including technicians not wearing sterile latex gloves at all times, not documenting the order in which the evidence was collected, and placing collected blood swatches in plastic containers instead of paper, which resulted in the samples degrading. It was even discovered that a DNA analyst had accidentally gotten blood from O.J.'s sample on his lab gloves just before testing some blood drops found at the crime scene.

Left: On Tuesday, October 3, 1995, O.J. Simpson stands in court with his lawyers as he is found not guilty of murdering his ex-wife Nicole Brown Simpson and her friend Ron Goldman. DNA mishandling made many pieces of evidence unusable in court.

Nevertheless, evidence pointed to O.J. as the killer. After a heavily media-covered slow-speed chase in a friend's Ford Bronco, Simpson was arrested for murder on June 17, 1994. Five days later, Simpson stood in court and pled, "Absolutely, 100 percent not guilty." Six months later, the murder trial began. It wasn't long before DNA results were presented to the judge and jury.

Because of all the mishandling of the evidence, the DNA evidence was questioned over and over. During the trial, the prosecution and the defense began their "DNA wars." Three different labs conducted analyses on the collected samples. The labs found O.J.'s DNA in drops of blood at the crime scene, as well as traces of Nicole and Ron's blood in Simpson's car and house. However, the defense pointed out that the police may have accidentally or purposefully planted the DNA evidence. They also proved many mishandlings and possible contaminations of the evidence. Although other evidence, including the bloody glove and socks, pointed to O.J. as the murderer, Simpson was found not guilty in criminal court.

DNA Use Today

The O.J. Simpson trial presented a vivid description of what *not* to do when collecting and processing crime scene DNA. The case resulted in stronger rules, procedures, and training for crime scene investigators.

DNA's importance in forensic science is certain. John Hicks, deputy assistant director of the FBI Laboratory Division, Washington, D.C., stated in *The Scientist* magazine, "Today, the application of DNA typing technology to criminal investigations is perhaps the most significant forensic breakthrough of the century."

DNA is vitally important in finding and convicting criminals. Cases of murder, manslaughter, rape, and aggravated assault (serious bodily injury) often use DNA to pinpoint the felons, and to prove their guilt in court. Many wrongdoers are behind bars because they cannot hide from this valuable forensic tool.

Below: A forensic scientist processes DNA samples. The use of DNA testing has resulted in more criminals being caught and innocent defendants being freed.

DNA profiling is also invaluable in reversing wrongful convictions. The "Innocence Project," a New York-based, non-profit legal clinic begun in 1992, helps inmates who claim to have been wrongly found guilty and are serving time in jail.

Left: James Tillman spent more than 16 years in prison for a crime he didn't commit. Beside him stands Karen Goodrow of the Innocence Project, a group dedicated to seeing wrongfully convicted people released from prison by using DNA proof. In 1989, Tillman was convicted of kidnapping, rape, and assault. In 1990, DNA testing was conducted on the evidence. However, the process was not yet advanced enough. Finally, in 2005, with Goodrow's help, additional testing was completed, proving that Tillman was innocent. He was released in 2006.

Mistaken identity, lab error, and even false confessions caused these innocent people to be convicted of crimes they didn't commit. Law students, with the supervision of licensed attorneys, handle the cases. DNA testing is conducted on whatever biological evidence is still available from a case. Over the course of 15 years, the Innocence Project has used DNA testing to free 208 innocent people.

There is no doubt that law enforcement agencies will continue to use DNA testing to protect the innocent and identify the guilty.

GLOSSARY

AUTORADIOGRAPH — A photographic film of an image created by radioactively treating an object and recording the radiation coming from that object.

BLOOD TYPE — Every human has one of four blood types: A, B, AB, or O. The type, which is inherited from a person's parent, depends on the substances found or missing from red blood cells.

CONTAMINATE — The adding of another substance or substances causing the original material to become impure or unclean.

CRIMINOLOGIST — A person who studies crimes and criminals to understand how these people think and behave. A criminologist's work helps law enforcement find and capture criminals by predicting what a criminal may do in certain situations.

DEFENDANT — A person, business, or government entity (such as a corporation or town) accused of doing something wrong. In a court trial, defendants try to defend themselves against the charge or charges placed against them.

DISTILLED WATER — Pure water that is free from dissolved salts and other chemicals.

DNA — DNA is short for the scientific term Deoxyribonucleic Acid. In living things, DNA is the material inside the center of every cell that forms genes. This material is inherited from an individual's parents. Except for identical twins, each person's DNA is unique to that person. Identical twins have identical DNA.

EVIDENCE — Objects, and sometimes information, that help prove the details and facts in a legal investigation.

GENETICIST — A scientist who studies relationship between genes and the traits that are inherited from a parent to a child or from one living thing to another.

HAIR FOLLICLE — A sac from which a hair grows. The follicle is lined with a collection of cells and contains the root of a hair. It is the root of the hair, not the hair itself, which contains DNA.

IMMIGRATION — The movement of a person or persons from one area into another. To settle in a new country.

PERPETRATOR — A person who commits a crime.

POROUS — An object or substance that is full of pores, allowing gasses and liquids to pass through. Examples of some porous materials include paper, wood, and clay.

PROSECUTOR — A person who brings charges of wrongdoing against another person, business, or government entity (defendant). These charges may lead to a trial taking place. During this trial, the prosecution tries to prove that the defendant is guilty.

SEMEN — The white-colored male reproductive fluid.

Above: A swab is used to collect DNA from a piece of evidence.

INDEX